Silenc

Abortion in a Virtuous Society

Christi
This one is my
labor of love.

Douglas V. Gibbs

Constitution Association Press: Murrieta, California

To my mom, who chose life when the circumstances were difficult.

ALSO BY DOUGLAS V. GIBBS

25 Myths of the United States Constitution

The Basic Constitution: An Examination of the Principles
and Philosophies of the United States Constitution

CONTENTS

ACKNOWLEDGMENTS

I would like to thank Andrea Yim for her dedication to carry out her husband's vision at pro-jectlife.com ("Speak up for people who cannot speak for themselves. Protect the rights of all who are helpless." Proverbs 31:8); Survivors of the Abortion Holocaust (www.survivors.la) and their event "International Pro-Life Youth Conference"; Birth Choice Temecula (www.birthchoicetemecula.com); and all of the folks fighting for the lives of innocent children worldwide. Your conferences, speeches, websites, and other efforts, inspired me to write this book.

INTRODUCTION

Twenty-one days after conception an ultrasound may detect a heartbeat.

An unborn baby's brain is "patterned" by four weeks as the earliest "rudiment" of the human nervous system forms.

By week seven the fingers and toes are clearly defined.

At eight weeks an unborn baby has the capacity to feel pain.

At eight weeks after conception the fingerprints are evident.

At nine weeks an unborn baby can swallow, and stick out his or her tongue.

At ten weeks an unborn baby begins to suck his or her thumb, and get hiccups.

This book discusses an issue that we are told we should not be talking about. In politics, according to conventional wisdom, taking a pro-life stance regarding abortion is a losing position. Consultants plead with politicians and political candidates to stay away from the social issues. Those issues, they tell them, are poison, and must be avoided at all cost if you even wish to succeed in politics.

The advice being given to our representatives and electoral candidates is in error. . . by design.

The supporters of the barbarity of abortion do not want the opposition talking about the slaughter of millions of unborn babies because in reality it is not a losing issue for the pro-life movement, or for the politicians that support the pro-life movement's efforts. If the truth about abortion was to ever get out there, it would be a losing issue for the purveyors of death.

Most of the activists of the pro-life movement that I have talked to have told me that it was when they realized the true barbarity of the practice of abortion, they became active members of the pro-life movement. For many, it was images of mangled bodies pulled from the birth canal piece by piece, or bloody babies lying on the table gasping for breath. For others, it was the descriptions of those abortions, the reality that poisons and murderous devices are used to ensure the baby dies before the mother realizes what she has done.

Horrifying accounts such as we experienced while we followed the Kermit Gosnell abortion trial in

Philadelphia remind us of how sickening the practice of abortion is, and how evil the people involved in it truly are.

Names like Margaret Sanger and Francis Galton remind us of the racist nature of abortion, and how these people saw it as an important tool in their eugenics agenda. The drive to create a master race included the killing of "the feeble-minded, idiots, morons" and "to cut down on the rapid multiplication of the unfit and undesirable at home," which included members of races Sanger viewed as unfit for the genetic pool, such as blacks, and Asians.

In Rome, when that great empire had departed from the height of its greatness, when immorality was collapsing the civilization from within, it became legal to leave your undesired child on the side of the road to die from exposure, if the child was under two years of age.

In the Old Testament, accounts of peoples giving their children to the sacrifices of fire for sensuality and convenience are followed by rebukes from God, and punishment for the Israelites that adopted the practice.

November 1, 2014, famed Hollywood actress Ellen Barkin proclaimed on Twitter that, "News flash…a fetus cannot talk. It is not a person. Not even a baby, not even an infant. Nope. Sorry." Was she suggesting that babies that have not learned to talk yet are also viable targets for death?

Cass Sunstein, President Barack Obama's Regulatory Czar in 2009, compared unborn babies to parasites in his 1993 book, *The Partial Constitution*. He wrote, "Restrictions on abortion, surrogacy and free availability of pornography are troublesome."

In 2002, Mr. Sunstein was caught on video placing animals above the lives of the unborn, as well as babies in the first months of their life outside the womb, while quoting from Bentham's 1789 primer, "Introduction to the Principles of Morals and Legislation," written just after slaves had been freed by the French but were still held captive in the British dominions:

"The day may come, when the rest of the animal creation may acquire those rights which never could have been withholden from them but by the hand of tyranny. The French have already discovered that the blackness of the skin is no reason why a human being should be abandoned without redress to the caprice of a tormentor."

Sunstein continued quoting the author, saying, "A full-grown horse or dog is beyond comparison a more rational, as well as a more conversable animal, than an infant of a day or a week or even a month, old. But suppose the case were otherwise."

In 2003, Sunstein wrote in a book review that there

is no moral concern regarding cloning human beings since human embryos, which develop into a baby, are "only a handful of cells."

Cass Sunstein, along with his mentor, Peter Singer, have written, and verbalized, their belief that abortion should be allowed after birth up to two years of age.

~ ~ ~

Proverbs 8:36 records God saying, "All they that hate Me love death."

"Only a virtuous people are capable of freedom."
-- Benjamin Franklin

"Our Constitution was made only for a moral and religious people. It is wholly inadequate to the government of any other." -- John Adams

"[The adoption of the Constitution] will demonstrate as visibly the finger of Providence as any possible event in the course of human affairs can ever designate it." -- George Washington

"A well-instructed people alone can be permanently a free people." -- James Madison

"The good sense of the people will always be found to be the best army. They may be led astray for a moment, but will soon correct themselves."
-- Thomas Jefferson

1 – THE LAW OF THE LAND

The United States Constitution was written to create a federal government, and then limit it to only functions it was designed to handle. The federal government was established to operate in a manner to protect the union, and State sovereignty. This means that all external issues, and conflicts between the States, are powers that belong to the federal government, while all internal issues belong to the States.

The English Colonies developed as independent entities, handling their local issues at the local level. The British Empire, until the approach of the American Revolution, left local affairs to local magistrates.

The Americans realized that local issues are best addressed by local government. A large, centralized government, when imposing its authority onto local issues, begins to micromanage the citizenry, dictating to the people the actions of their daily lives. When tyranny rises in such a manner, it is not long before death becomes the order of the day.

The United States Constitution extends those principles of self-governance to the States by only authorizing the federal government with certain powers. Those powers are expressly granted in the text of the United States Constitution. Abortion, medical procedures, or any issue regarding individual persons in regards to whether or not those individuals should be allowed to live or die, are not addressed in the Constitution, and therefore are not within the authorities granted to the federal government. As per the 10th Amendment, those same issues are not prohibited to the States. Therefore, abortion is an issue that is legally supposed to be decided on a State-by-State basis.

Any federal court decisions striking down a State law regarding the issue of abortion, based on the principles and philosophies of the United States Constitution, are unconstitutional. The federal government has no legal authority regarding the issue. We, however, have been taught otherwise, and have come to falsely trust the lawmakers and judiciary regarding their handling of the issue of abortion.

We the People have the power to change the system, but can only do so if we are educated regarding the issue of abortion, understand the originally intended application of the United States Constitution, and approach the issue with a firm reliance on the protection of divine Providence.

2 – LONELY MOTEL

Somewhere near Carson, California; 1967

Tears rolled down her cheeks. The moisture from the hours of crying had long since drenched the otherwise delicate skin of the young woman who was viewing her high school years in the rearview mirror of her life.

Going home was not an option. She burned that bridge when she married a man nearly twice her age. With their high school graduation gowns hung away, all of her high school friends had lives of their own, either as students in college, or working a job to support their new adult lives.

Judy sat on the bed in a motel room wondering what she should do. How did she get herself into this mess? In the process of seeking a companion, mixed with a massive load of eye-stabbing rebellion against her parents, she now found herself alone, with no money, and no hope, in a dumpy motel room. Her baby boy, a precious bundle in the earliest stages of life, lay sleeping on the bed. Quiet. Peaceful. Sweet.

He was her reason for living. Her loneliness would be unbearable if it was not for that sweet child lying on the bed as the noise of traffic flowed by outside the heavily draped windows of the room. Sirens blared in the distance, and the people of the Los Angeles suburb passed by in their busy lives without even knowing that a teenager was struggling with the consequences of her decisions inside the old motel.

Abortion may, or may not have, crossed her mind. Suicide danced in her head on occasion, but the sweet baby on the bed kept her from making such a horrific decision. The deluge of tears continued as she sat there wrapped in fear, and loneliness.

Judy, if she wanted to, could have blamed her terrible circumstances on her overbearing mother who expected perfection at every turn. The older woman punished Judy for every little action, blaming the girl for the slightest inconsistency in their household. The onslaught had brought the young woman to wrath, rebellion, and rejection of her home life.

Judy could also, just as easily, blame her dad, who lived in a marriage he really didn't want to be in, and who constantly packed his bags and left at the slightest opportunity, only to send for his family later when guilt caught up with him.

She could have easily said to herself, "it's all their

fault," and their inability to be proper parents could easily have taken the blame for the reason she was in this predicament. But Judy knew better. She had made her own decisions. She made her own bed, and now the results of her actions were upon her with the worst kind of punishment she could imagine. Loneliness, save for the companionship of her sweet baby boy.

A concerned high school friend came to visit Judy at the dirty motel, and they cried together. Then, by the grace of God, Judy found a way to move forward, to take the incredibly impossible situation in which she found herself and leave it behind her. She placed it all in God's hands. Regardless of the chaos of her childhood, she knew that Jesus was with her, carrying her when life was at its worst.

Eventually, Judy grew beyond the fear, and she married a man that came to love her sweet son as she did. The marriage continues on to this day. Judy, and her husband, have two more children of their own since the day they exchanged wedding vows. The three kids, the boy that provided hope in Judy's time of sorrow, and his younger half-sister and half-brother, have grown up, married, and have children of their own. The oldest, the precious gift from Heaven that was literally a red-headed step-child, has been married for over thirty years, has two children of his own, and six beautiful grandchildren that reminds him every time he has the blessed opportunity to spend time with them that children are precious, blessed, and a gift from God.

Judy is my mother. The sweet little boy was me.

3 – LOOKING BACK

I have always wondered what the consequences would have been, aside from the obvious, if my mother had realized, while pregnant with me, that the marriage to the older man was not going to work out, and that she may be too young to have a child. In today's society, aborting the baby that was me, while I was still in the womb, would have been the expected thing to do. We are told that the murderous practice of abortion saves lives, that children who are brought into the world under poor conditions, or by mothers not seen as being capable of properly taking care of a child, should be mercilessly put to death while in their earliest stage of development as a person.

Those that advocate legal abortion existed long before the time of my birth, but the issue was on the verge of exploding as my mom sat on that bed in a cheap motel pondering the choices of her young life. A little more than a year after my birth, on June 14, 1967, California Governor Ronald Reagan, a man that would later become known for his pro-life stance as President of the United States in the

1980s, signed the *Therapeutic Abortion Act, Health and Safety Code*. The new California law legalized the termination of pregnancy by a physician, in an accredited hospital, when there was a specific finding that there was a substantial risk that its continuation would "gravely impair the physical or mental health of the mother," or when the pregnancy resulted from rape or incest. The law set a limit for abortion at the 20th week of pregnancy.

Societal response to the new law, much to the distress of the Governor, was that the number of abortions in California increased dramatically. Reagan signed the bill with the addition of some added "protections," because the Legislature was set to override a veto in case he decided to reject the proposed legislation.

Sections of the California law were struck down by the California State Supreme Court in 1969 because the provisions were "vague and uncertain," and deprived the unborn children of their right to due process. More importantly, in the eyes of those that support the concept of "case law," the ruling set a precedent rejecting the concept that a woman's "right" to end the life of the unborn child in her womb takes priority over the life of the unborn.

In 1972, the California Supreme Court invalidated nearly all of the provisions of the Therapeutic Abortion Act signed by Governor Reagan in 1967, agreeing with the 1969 decision that the language was vague, and due process was not guaranteed.

Later, during the same year, mere months before *Roe v. Wade* was decided on January 22, 1973, while seeking financial privacy, the people of California added to their State Constitution the right of "privacy" to the other inalienable rights of individuals enumerated in Article I, Section I, of the State Constitution. The addition to the State Constitution recognized that any rights in California's Constitution are not dependent on those guaranteed in the U.S. Constitution. The State amendment was an attempt to protect financial privacy, and the constitutional concept of State Sovereignty. The addition to the State Constitution was a noble move based on a constitutionally sound argument. The supporters of legalized abortion, however, used the result of the California vote for financial privacy for their own agenda, claiming California's "right to privacy" included a guarantee of abortion rights.

January 22, 1973, the United States Supreme Court ruled on *Roe v. Wade,* and its companion case, *Doe v. Bolton*, and the perceived result of the federal high court overturning a State law on a constitutionally defined State issue, was that every anti-abortion statute at the State level was rendered unconstitutional. In other words, the ruling did not merely strike down the Texas law banning abortion, but any anti-abortion law in any State. The ruling established that protection of a nonviable fetus could not be justified as a matter of law. If the unborn child could not survive on its own outside the womb, the baby is not a person, and no laws could be passed to restrict a woman's "right" to abort the child.

The court added that if the child is viable, if the unborn baby could survive outside the womb without assistance, States could pass laws restricting abortions of these viable fetuses, but only with maximum justification. What resulted was the birth of the abortion culture, the rise of abortion mills, and the emergence of abortion-on-demand through the use of protections created by the federal court system under the guise that killing one's unborn children is a constitutional right.

Justice Harry Blackmun, in his 7-2 majority opinion of the ruling that decided *Roe v. Wade*, pointed out that "personhood" is the key. However, simply declaring personhood begins at conception may not be enough to sway a court system determined to do everything it can to stand against the morals and traditions of America's founding.

Language such as that presented in Missouri's statutory preamble enacted in the 1980s, when harkening back to Blackmun's opinion, may be effective in the effort to protect the unborn by labeling these children as "persons." The language in Missouri's statutory preamble reads:

1. The general assembly of [Missouri] finds that:

(1) The life of each human being begins at

conception;

(2) Unborn children have protectable interests in life, health, and well-being;

(3) The natural parents of unborn children have protectable interests in the life, health, and well-being of their unborn child.

After the *Roe v. Wade* ruling in 1973, the decisions of the California State Supreme Court regarding the right to due process and the right to life of the unborn child were no longer considered legal. All amendments to the law Ronald Reagan signed in 1967 were no longer accepted. The only part of California's *Therapeutic Abortion Act* that remained constitutional, according to those that support the concept of constitutionality based on the opinions of judges, and the complicated web of case law, was that a physician by law must perform the abortion.

Though I was born long before *Roe v. Wade* in 1973, the Supreme Court ruling that opened the floodgates of America's modern day genocide was not the first time the issue of abortion had been visited. The debate regarding abortion existed long before *Roe v. Wade*.

Concerns regarding abortion in the United States date as far back as into the early 1800s.

In 1821, America's first statutory abortion regulation was enacted in Connecticut. The law was designed to protect women from abortion inducement through poison administered after the fourth month of pregnancy.

In 1856, Dr. Horatio Storer established a national push by the American Medical Association (AMA) to end legal abortion. During the mid-1800s, first trimester abortion was legal or a misdemeanor in most States.

In 1873, The Comstock Act banned the dissemination of information about abortion and birth control by mail.

In 1890, abortion became defined as a medical procedure that was mostly regulated by statutes advocated by the AMA. Abortion, at that point, was usually only permitted upon conferral of one or more physicians who believed the procedure was necessary to preserve the life of the mother.

In 1939, the founder of Planned Parenthood, and a proponent for abortion and forced sterilization in the United States for the purpose of exterminating "undesirable" people, Margaret Sanger, proposed that abortion and forced sterilization must be used to support the agenda of those that defended eugenics. The 1939 Negro Project was designed to convince the black population to participate in the program, and for the black population to accept abortion as an important tool for their well-being as a segment of society.

Sanger's Birth Control Policy included the "racial hygiene theory." Racial hygiene theory, according to Sanger, would "cleanse" humanity of the "morons," "human weeds," and the "feeble-minded" that negatively affected our populations. In 1922, in Sanger's book, *The Pivot of Civilization*, she wrote, "Birth Control, which has been criticized as negative and destructive, is really the greatest and most truly eugenic method, and its adoption as part of the program of Eugenics would immediately give a concrete and realistic power to that science... as the most constructive and necessary of the means to racial health." (Page 189)

Sanger also wrote that she believed "The emergency problem of segregation and sterilization must be faced immediately. Every feeble-minded girl or woman of the hereditary type, especially of the moron class, should be segregated during the reproductive period.... we prefer the policy of immediate sterilization, of making sure that parenthood is absolutely prohibited to the feeble-minded." (Pages 101-102)

For Sanger, the purpose in promoting birth control was "to create a race of thoroughbreds," as she wrote in the *Birth Control Review*, November 1921 (p. 2).

The drive for racial purification included the extermination of what she considered to be lesser races, including blacks. "We do not want word to go out that we want to exterminate the Negro population," she said, "if it ever occurs to any of their more rebellious members."

Sanger's writings and influence led to the passage of segregation laws, sterilization laws, and the Immigration Act of 1924 that included a provision excluding from entry any alien who by virtue of race or nationality was ineligible for citizenship.

Despite Sanger's efforts, the abortion issue from a legal standpoint remained as it had been – illegal unless the medical community recognized, on a case by case basis, that it was absolutely necessary to save the life of the mother.

Though the issue seemed to be resolved in the United States, underground, a culture of death targeting the innocent lives of unborn children, still existed. A number of illegal abortionists performed the procedure in what today those that advocate for legalized abortion call "back alley abortions." Europe, however, remained intent upon moving towards making abortion more prevalent, establishing methods designed to make the killing of the unborn "safer." In 1961, vacuum aspiration-style abortion spread throughout Europe, and it didn't take long before the pro-abortion segment of American Society caught on to the idea.

In 1963, The Society for Human Abortion (SHA) was established in San Francisco. The organization, designed to promote and legalize "elective abortion" without "harassment," supported the repeal of all anti-abortion laws. The SHA challenged anti-abortion laws by openly providing information on abortion through providing speakers and literature to libraries, medical schools, physicians, family planning agencies, and individuals. The information avalanche also included providing their view of abortion through the publishing of a quarterly newsletter. In 1968 the SHA maintained a free Post-Abortion Care Center (PACC), which was sponsored by the American Humanist Association. SHA disbanded in 1975.

In addition to the SHA, a parallel organization was established to safeguard the SHA's tax-free educational status, while enabling the group to carry out underground activities. The Association to Repeal Abortion Laws (ARAL) made referrals to abortion specialists, while preparing and disseminating printed material about specialists and about self-induced abortion. The ARAL also held classes on abortion-related laws, provided information on Mexican abortion specialists, and sought to teach pregnant mothers on self-induced abortion techniques. For a small donation, pregnant women received a kit prepared by ARAL containing annotated lists of abortion specialists in Mexico, Japan, Puerto Rico, and other countries, instructions for going through customs, an evaluation form to be returned to ARAL after completion of the abortion, summaries of laws, and directions for self-induced abortion. The evaluations were used to update the list of abortion specialists.

When California was legalizing abortion with Governor Reagan's signature in 1967, abortion was classified a felony in 49 states and Washington, D.C. In California, Dr. Leon Belous was convicted for referring a woman to an illegal abortionist, which was the case that led to the 1969 California Supreme Court decision that ignited the battle over abortion in that State.

4 – AN EMPTY GRAVE

The young couple met in high school, and after graduation, their love blossomed into something nobody could understand. Their love was deeper than anyone could explain. Life after graduation, for the young man, presented opportunities he had been waiting for. He was ready to be his own man, an independent individual making his own path in life. It was time to make some money, and begin the process of creating a scenario where he could afford to marry his girlfriend, and for them to begin their life together.

Shortly after her young life as an adult began, the young lady realized she was pregnant. She was frightened. She knew they weren't ready for a family, yet, and she knew that her boyfriend was raised in a Christian household, and would probably be against her having an abortion.

Though her own family were not advocates for legalized abortion, the young woman had been taught in school that she had the *right* to make decisions for her own body, and it was none of her boyfriend's business if she decided to keep the child, or not. The "fetus" was in *her* body, not his. He wouldn't have to carry the baby for nine months, and he would not be the one slaving throughout the day caring for the little parasite.

She had the abortion without his knowledge, intent on keeping it a secret for the rest of her life. He didn't need to know, and she wasn't going to tell him.

Her guilt, however, overtook her, and when she told him that she had terminated the life of their unborn child, his anger overtook him. How could he marry a woman that did not see a baby as a blessing? How could he trust her with anything, ever again?

As he walked out the door forever, he said over his shoulder, "You didn't even give the baby the dignity of a headstone."

"It was *my right* to choose," she screamed.

He never came back.

5 – DEFINITION OF A RIGHT

The claim that abortion is a "woman's *right* to choose" seems to forget that there are two other people in the equation. What about the rights of the father as a parent? What about the rights of the child whose death is being inflicted without he or she having any *choice* in the matter?

Those that advocate legalized abortion have used the Constitution to support their agenda, misconstruing the original intent of the document, and the definitions of the language used by the Founding Fathers.

In the Declaration of Independence the founders explained that our rights are "self-evident," and that they are "endowed" by our "Creator." When listing a few examples of our rights, the document proclaims that "among these are Life, Liberty, and the pursuit of Happiness."

The inspiration for the definition of what is considered *a right*, and what is not considered *a right*, comes from the concept of Natural Rights. In the first paragraph of the Declaration of Independence, our rights are described as being "entitled" by the "Laws of Nature and of Nature's God."

In the final sentence of the Declaration of Independence, the signers again refer to the importance of God in the establishment of the American experiment. The final sentence reads, "And for the support of this Declaration, with a firm reliance on the protection of **divine Providence**, we mutually pledge to each other our Lives, our Fortunes and our sacred Honor."

Divine Providence is defined as, "The care and superintendence which God exercises over His creatures."

The Constitution does not grant us our rights. Our rights are not guaranteed by the Constitution, nor protected by the Bill of Rights. The task of standing against oppression, and restraining government from compromising our God-given rights, belongs to us.

Understanding that our rights are important to us in American society, largely due to the fact that a number of those rights are enumerated in the Bill of Rights of the United States Constitution, those that support issues like elective abortion have connived that to ensure their agenda is achieved by mis-defining their goals as *human rights*.

The *right* to abortion is considered to be a part of the much larger umbrella of women's *rights*. In recent arguments, the supporters of legalized abortion call terminating the life of an unborn child a "reproductive *right*." Women who advocate legal abortion proclaim, "I have a *right* to do with my own body what I choose." Everything associated with the murderous practices of abortion mills has been labeled a *right*.

As explained in the Declaration of Independence, and John Locke's writings regarding Natural Law, our rights are God-given. We have been endowed with our rights by the Creator, and those rights are "self-evident."

In a virtuous society, set moral standards are an important part of the proper functioning of the culture. Right and wrong are "self-evident," because the citizens understand that their individual rights were established by God. Therefore, not only is it tyrannical for government to try to regulate, compromise, or take away those rights, but that government has no part in defining what those rights are.

Since our rights are *God-given*, that means that the definition of a right includes God. A right, then, is unalienable, possessed by the individual by virtue of birth, and therefore, to be defined as a right, it must be sanctioned by God. If God, in other words, would not approve of the alleged right, then it is not a right.

Abortion is the termination of the life of an unborn child while developing in the womb. Abortion is the taking of human life, for Scripture recognizes that life begins at conception. According to Psalms 139:13, God fashions us while we are in our mother's womb. Jeremiah was called to be a prophet before he was born according to Jeremiah 1:5. The Apostle Paul was similarly called by God while he was still an unborn child (Galatians 1:15). John The Baptist leaped in his mother's womb when the voice of Mary, the mother of Jesus Christ, was heard (Luke 1:44). The equality of all babies in the womb is explained in Job 31:15 where it is written, "Did not He Who made me in the womb make them? Did not the same One fashion us in the womb?"

Our time in the womb is nothing more than a stage of our development as a person that continues through adulthood. The personhood of babies is not only established in biblical text, but so is the blessed opportunity to be with child. The practice of abortion must be unthinkable to people of God. The idea of a mother killing her own child is an abomination, a disgrace, and an evil. The Old Testament is filled with passages of women yearning for children. Babies were considered a gift from God. Women prayed to not be barren.

God condemned Israelites that offered their children as sacrifices to the heathen god Molech. In Leviticus 20:2, God condemned those that offered their children to the fires of sacrifice to a god of *sensuality and convenience*. When Israel was in Egypt, the Pharaoh forced the Israelites to kill their newborn babies, a mandate that was looked upon as the height of cruel oppression (Exodus 1:15-22).

Abortion is a terrible blot on our society. The advocates of killing babies while they remain in the womb do so for the purpose of *sensuality and convenience*, as did the worshipers of Molech. The value of life has been cheapened. The life of a baby, once considered a blessing and a precious gift from God, is now called a mistake, an inconvenience that can be terminated at will by an industry driven by an ungodly political agenda. Abortion is driven by ill-gotten wealth, power, sexual perversion and sexual predators. Abortions are carried out by doctors willing to kill in a barbaric manner when the very definition of their profession is about saving lives.

How can a righteous woman turn against her own children to destroy them?

When a woman enters an abortion clinic, two hearts are beating. After the procedure, only her heart is beating, and the blood of the baby has been spilled. God does not sanction the practice of abortion, but instead views it as the height of pagan barbarity.

If God does not sanction an activity, the proponents of that activity can call it a right all they want, but that does not make it so. Natural rights are God-given, therefore, abortion is not a right. Abortion is simply a selfish act of murder against innocent lives that are guilty of nothing more than existing.

6 – IN THE CLINIC

She awakened early in the morning to stand in line at the abortion clinic, waiting for the doors to open. She just wanted to get the procedure over with, and then go on with her life. The "thing" growing in her stomach was a reminder of all of her mistakes, and the jerk she had allowed herself to have sex with. Out of sight, out of mind. She was determined to have the procedure, and forget about the mass of cells in her body forever.

Nearby, a mobile clinic was parked, and the people in charge of the vehicle offered a free pre-clinic screening. What could it hurt? She had to wait until the doors opened, anyway, and a number of women had already gone into the van to receive a medical check-up.

Her nervousness regarding the procedure she was determined to go through began to well up in her chest as she laid back on the table, and the worker lifted her shirt to expose her slightly bulging tummy. The woman attending the pregnant girl applied a kind of jelly on the mother's skin, and then began the ultrasound. The young woman that began her day determined to have an abortion watched the screen, recognizing the shape of a human body, watching as the tiny body inside her flinched, and moved. At one point, even though she knew it was impossible, she could have sworn the little face turned towards the screen to look at her.

After the ultrasound, the medical assistant walked out of the cubicle, leaving the young mother to her thoughts.

She pictured what the life of that baby may be like. What would she look like when she was born? Would she have the same color hair as Mommy? What would be her first word? When would she take her first step? Would she be nervous on her first day of school? Would she be better at math, or reading? How old would she be when she fell in love? Would she go to college? When would she marry? What would her husband look like? How many babies would she have?

The girl in the clinic had watched the entire life of her unborn baby flash before her eyes, and now all she could do was lay there on the table, crying. After seeing her baby on the ultrasound, she decided that there was no force in the world that could convince her to abort her baby, now.

7 – THE NUMBERS

In the United States, about half of all pregnancies are unintended. Four out of ten unintended pregnancies end in abortion. There are about 1.21 million abortions in the United States every twelve months. Each year about 2% of all women aged 15-44 have an abortion, and of all of abortions during the year, about 47% of them have had at least one previous abortion. The United States has the highest abortion rate (19.4 per 1,000) of any western industrialized nation.

61% of abortions are performed on babies in the first 9 weeks of pregnancy. 18% are slaughtered between 9 and 10 weeks. 10% between 11 and 12 weeks. 11% of babies are aborted beyond the first trimester.

The younger the adult woman, the more likely she is going to have an abortion. A third of all abortions are performed on women between the ages of 20 and 24. A quarter of all abortions take place on women between the ages of 25 and 29. More than half of all abortions are carried out on women in their twenties.

Over a third of all terminated pregnancies are black, and in New York City more black babies die from abortion than are born alive. Black women are five times more likely to abort than white women. Planned Parenthood has located 80% of its abortion clinics in minority neighborhoods, targeting minorities for abortion, keeping the racist dreams of Margaret Sanger alive.

The number of abortions has been on a steady decline since 1980.

In opinion polls, the pro-life movement has increased to a majority in recent years, after claiming only 33% of the population in 1995.

On the front lines have been mobile units, counseling centers, and other health services designed to stop the deadly practice of abortion. These locations provide ultrasounds so that a woman considering abortion can see that the life inside her is in fact the precious life of a blessed person. Centers provide counseling to encourage women to choose life, and counseling for those traumatized because the agenda of death convinced them to end the life of their babies. It is about saving babies, saving lives, and encouraging women to love their children by keeping them.

After the birth, services to assist the woman with her child, or to assist in adoption services, are often also available.

All to save babies. All to save the lives of their children.

Prayer, sidewalk counseling, mobile clinics, and counseling centers have worked together to save thousands of babies, and sway public opinion. The war to end abortion in our lifetime, however, has only just begun. The dark forces of death use all tools available to them, including lies, hiding the real numbers, and using the courts to fight against the pro-life movement being able to reveal images of how barbaric the practice of abortion really is.

In December of 2014, the 4th U.S. Circuit Court of Appeals heard a case regarding a North Carolina law requiring women seeking an abortion to have an ultrasound of the unborn child performed. Proponents of the law say that requiring ultrasounds narrated by the physician provides crucial information to women before they make an irrevocable decision. The law, as it was written, requires physicians to perform an ultrasound, display the sonogram and describe the image of the baby to women seeking abortions. The narration by the doctor enables the patient to hear, even if they choose to avert their eyes, a description of the baby to better enable them to understand the gravity of their potential decision regarding the child in their womb.

The federal court upheld a district judge's decision

to unconstitutionally strike down the 2011 law. The ruling described the law as being unconstitutional because it forces doctors to voice the State's message discouraging the abortion procedure, a violation, according to the ruling, of the free speech clause of the First Amendment of the United States Constitution.

The law was originally passed by North Carolina's Republican dominated legislature, overriding a veto by Governor Beverly Perdue, a Democrat.

In the rulings by the federal judges, while indicating State governments cannot force their message discouraging abortion, the judges not only failed to recognize abortion as being solely a State issue, but they did not see their own rulings as being a case of the federal government forcing the State and physicians to voice the federal government's message encouraging abortion.

An appeal of the ruling by North Carolina is expected, which will take the case to the United States Supreme Court, using as their defense the fact that another federal appeals court recently upheld a similar ultrasound requirement in Texas. Refusal to adhere to the illegal federal rulings, a form of a State power known as *nullification*, by the State, has not been entertained as a consideration by North Carolina's lawmakers, but should be.

Pro-abortion groups call the federal court ruling against North Carolina a "major victory for women and sends a message to lawmakers across the country: It is unconstitutional for politicians to interfere in a woman's personal medical decisions about abortion."

Pro-life groups claim laws like the one in North Carolina are needed to help women make informed choices about abortion.

Barbara Holt, president of the pro-life organization, North Carolina Right to Life, said regarding the provisions of the law in question, "This would give her an opportunity to pause and really take into consideration what decision she's making. We have a right that trumps free speech, and that's our unalienable right to life."

As the fight progresses, the reality is that the forces of death are not going away quietly, despite that fact that the percentage of people that consider themselves to be pro-life is increasing by percentage of the population. Abortion may very well be abolished in our lifetime, but as the abortionists realize their agenda of death is in trouble, their efforts will intensify.

8 – PIECES

"An RN left a Detroit abortion clinic recently. When she called me asking about our ministry, I asked her what it was that prompted her call. She said to me, 'I just can't do it anymore. I can't look at one more jar of these baby's body parts.'" - Abby Johnson, public Facebook page, April 30, 2014

"It was definitely gruesome. You could make out what a fetus could look like, tiny feet, lungs… It's a lot more invasive than I thought. A papaya doesn't bleed and scream. Women do." - Medical student Lesley Wojick.

"The procedure is easy," she told herself. So why was she so nervous? In medical school, she learned how easy the procedure is by practicing suction abortion on a papaya. "The instruments are designed," she tried to convince herself, "to make the procedure simple, and easy."

The patient had been given a medicine to partially dilate the cervix the night before. Now, the doctor was forcing her to participate in performing the abortion, or else she would lose her job as a nursing assistant. As a Christian, the very idea of terminating the innocent life of an unborn baby was appalling to her, but she needed the job.

Careful deliberation brought her to the conclusion that she couldn't go through with it. This was the last straw. She would be quitting. However, to survive, she needed to find a new job *before* resigning. So, with much fear and dread, she knew she had to participate in performing the abortion procedure to keep her job at least a little while. With a rise of internal horror, but unable to get out of it without placing herself into a financially detrimental position, she decided to assist the doctor in the barbaric procedure. She had heard of the methods, and the gruesome details, but no story she had heard regarding abortion ever properly prepared her for what she was going to experience next.

The baby to be aborted was in his second trimester, and the physician elected to use *dilation and extraction* method of abortion. The baby was partially delivered, leaving the head inside the womb since the head was too large to be easily extracted through the cervix. The doctor pierced the skull, sucking the brain out through a tube, collapsing the skull, and then delivering the remainder of the baby.

The body was removed prior to the collapsing of the skull, but removed from inside the womb piece by piece, purposely dismembered in utero with forceps, because the body still intact would be too difficult to pull through the cervical opening.

The cervical opening was small because it had to be forced open by laminaria, which are sticks made of seaweed that are inserted into a woman's cervix in order to open it. The laminaria absorb fluid and gradually stretch open the cervix, often left in overnight. Forcibly opening the cervix by instrumentation later in a pregnancy can permanently damage the cervix so severely that any later attempt to carry a child to term would likely end in miscarriage. Laminaria is normally used for a late-term abortion procedure.

That evening, the nursing assistant went home, traumatized by what she had seen. "Surely," she thought to herself, not all procedures are carried out like this." She knew that abortion is horrific, but what she saw was a complete disregard for the life of the child.

Online, she located a website authored by a former nursing assistant. The woman on the web, horrified by what she had experienced in an abortion mill, had not only departed from the abortion industry, but had become a pro-life advocate, completely changing her political associations and positions.

She read about a number of abortions performed past 26 weeks of pregnancy, on healthy babies with strong heartbeats and well defined human features. The doctor used an ultrasound screen to watch what he was doing, going into the woman's uterus with forceps and grabbing the baby's legs. He pulled the legs into the birth canal, delivering the body and arms, all the way up to the neck. Then, while the baby's head remained inside his mother, and the baby's body moving in the birth canal and his little fingers were clasping together while kicking his feet, the physician took a pair of scissors and inserted them into the back of the baby's head. Then he stuck a high-powered suction tube into the hole and sucked the baby's brains out.

After pulling the head out of the young woman, the doctor cut the umbilical cord, removed the placenta, and threw the baby in a pan, along with the placenta and the instruments he'd used, like it was yesterday's garbage. The baby moved, but another nurse said it was just reflexes.

The participants in the abortion industry call the babies "fetuses" because they want to encourage an image of the babies being just a blob of cells, or a mass of something that is something other than an unborn child. The babies being aborted, however, are nothing of the sort, and when some of the doctors and nurses realize that the bodies they are discarding are the perfect little bodies of babies fashioned by the Creator, the image haunts them. It becomes very revealing, and their humanity finally takes over, and they turn away from the industry of death.

9 – HOUSE OF HORRORS

Pregnancy has become a commercial transaction.

Kermit Gosnell's abortion clinic in Philadelphia has become known as the "House of Horrors." Gosnell's 17-year career in abortion made him a millionaire, as he performed abortions in a squalid clinic that went uninspected by state officials, until he was convicted of first degree murder for killing three babies by snipping their necks with a pair of scissors after they were born alive. The country watched in horror as the testimony of former personnel from the clinic recounted the late-term abortion practices at the facility that has turned out to be not an exception to the rule among abortionists, but the norm.

The clinic was a cesspool of filth, filled with blood-stained equipment, crumbling walls, and body parts stored in jars, bags and bottles. In fact, Gosnell proudly displayed jars of severed babies' feet as trophies.

The Grand Jury Report regarding the Gosnell case

is filled with details of Gosnell's "House of Horrors," with Philadelphia District Attorney, R. Seth Williams, a Democrat, writing, "My comprehension of the English language can't adequately describe the barbaric nature of Dr. Gosnell."

D.A. Williams said the unspeakable conditions of the clinic that was inspected by the pro-abortion National Abortion Federation was never reported to authorities.

In addition to murdering babies born alive, Gosnell, who is black, made sure that his white "patients" were placed in the cleaner rooms while all others were placed in the filthy rooms. This way, according to the Grand Jury Report, it would be less likely that the white women would report the abortionist or his foul clinic.

In Houston, Texas, witness testimony regarding abortionist Douglas Karpen exposed that he aborted babies alive, often beyond twenty-four weeks of pregnancy, and then punctured the soft spot in their head, or impaled the stomach with a sharp instrument. Former employees also testified there were times when Karpen twisted the heads of babies off with his hands, or punctured their throat with his finger. Testimony consistently maintained that Karpen routinely aborted babies alive, and then murdered them "daily."

After the case was not allowed to move forward in

2013 because there was "insufficient evidence," the people involved with legally pursuing Karpen decided it was necessary to go public.

Ironically, Kermit Gosnell's trial interfered, so release of the information was delayed.

The emergence of the information regarding Karpen's gruesome abortion practices came at a time when the media was trying to convince the public that Kermit Gosnell was an anomaly. Karpen reminded the public that Gosnell was not an anomaly, and in reality, there are many more just like Gosnell, and Karpen performing late-term abortions, and murdering babies in a gruesome manner after the children are extracted from their mothers while still alive.

Abortionists across the country have been charged with murder, illegal drug trafficking, botched abortions, rape, and millions of dollars worth of Medicaid fraud. Planned Parenthood has been taken to court in State after State for millions of dollars of Medicaid fraud. Sexual predators continuously use abortion to hide their molestation of young girls, with abortion clinics routinely, and illegally, failing to report the young age of the patients. . . returning the young girls to their molesters after the procedure is complete. There are no "ethics" in a billion dollar industry that endangers, and ends, human life daily. When your business centers around killing human life, corruption in any other area is easy, and likely.

Tonya Reaves, a woman who received an abortion in Chicago, Illinois, was allowed to bleed for five and a half hours without the clinic ever calling for emergency services. Protecting the abortion agenda was more important than protecting, and saving, her life. On February 7, 2014, a court ordered Planned Parenthood to pay $2 million for the wrongful death of Tonya Reaves, but the money awarded will never make up for the death of the young woman, her unborn child, or the life the woman's young son will now have to live without his mother.

Over 55 million children and 400 women have died inside abortion clinics, and these are the ones actually reported. The true numbers may never be known as long as the media, and members of the political establishment, continue to cover up the truth in the name of playing the role of abortion advocate.

Despite the media working to cover up the truth, stories like that of Kermit Gosnell and Douglas Karpen still occasionally makes it into the headlines. Cases like Gosnell, Karpen, and that of the death of Tonya Reaves, typify the abortion industry. The horrors of these cases that shock so many are a daily occurrence in the abortion mills around the world, yet the proponents of abortion continue to support the slaughter of the unborn, and do whatever they can to protect the agenda of death.

10 – IGNORING THE SCREAMS

An elderly man's nightmares haunted him nightly. He dreamed of standing on railroad tracks, as the train bore down on him. The train was familiar, something from his memory, a distant memory from his childhood that would haunt him forever.

The telling of the old man's nightmare was first published by a woman named Penny Lea, and then the story was made into a film titled, "*Sing a Little Louder.*" The film tells the story of the old man standing on the train tracks, remembering when as a child, the train ran by his church, close enough to rattle the small building as it passed by during the morning service, always on time, always consistent.

Each Sunday morning, as the pastor delivered his sermon, the little boy that would become the elderly man standing on the tracks in his nightmares, pulled out his pocket watch, watching the minute hand as it approached the moment the train would come. The boy was watching to see if ever the train would be late, but it never was. Always, during the same journey through the pastor's latest sermon, the train approached, the ground rumbled, the church rattled, and the pastor would preach a little louder so that the congregation could hear him as the locomotive thundered by.

One morning, as the train approached, something happened that was out of the ordinary. The brakes were applied, and the train that normally rumbled by every morning, came to a stop in front of the small church. Mere feet from the entrance of the church, at the end of the walkway to the small fence that surrounded the church, sat the train, now unmoving from its travels. The boxcars, however, did not remain silent, and it was not long before the congregation recognized the sounds from the train.

The train tracks, and the church, resided in Germany during the Second World War. The German citizens in the church had heard rumors of people disappearing, of the Jews being rounded up and sent away, but they put it out of their mind, refusing to admit the horror of genocide existed. Now, as the stopped train sat on the tracks outside their church, people inside the boxcars heard the sermon being delivered by the pastor, and it encouraged them to cry out for help, hoping that someone would do something to save them from their final destination.

The screams multiplied as more people in the boxcars began to cry out. The pastor began to preach louder, as he would do on the mornings where the train passed by, but the screams of the people could still be heard. The cries of those imprisoned in the boxcars were still noticeable.

The pastor called on the choir to begin singing, hoping to drown out the reality of the cries outside. The choir reluctantly joined in, and as the cries outside became louder and louder, the pastor encouraged parishioners to join the singing. One by one members of the congregation arose from their seats, singing louder and louder to drown out the cries for help outside, hoping to protect their own ears from the horrors of the reality that existed mere feet from the entrance of their small church.

A woman reached for the hand of her son, but he was missing. The boy had left his spot at the pew, and was outside to see what the noise from the train was all about.

The boy that would become a man tortured by nightmares stood before the boxcar, staring at the faces between the wooden slats. A woman, recognizing the boy's fear, tried to calm him, asking from inside the boxcar, "What is your name?"

Unable to answer, the young German boy simply stood there, tears streaming down his cheeks, as his innocence was shed, and he realized the reality of what he was confronted with. The agenda of death was before him, committed by his own countrymen, against a people that were being used as a scapegoat for the troubles of a war-torn nation.

German soldiers walked along the tracks, laughing and talking as they stepped closer to the voices that cried out for help from the boxcar, and the little boy confronted with the reality of the prisoners on the train. His mother ran up behind him as the soldiers approached, seeing what the boy saw, looking into the eyes of the woman in the boxcar, and seeing the faces of her doomed companions.

The soldiers instructed her to take her child back into the church, as the choir and the congregation sang louder and louder to drown out the voices outside. The woman nodded, grabbed her son, and dragged him away, trying to forget what she saw, and eager to join the singing inside so that she too could drown out the truth that was so obvious all around her.

Despite the singing, the boy never forgot.

11 – SINGING LOUDER

The German people, after World War II, were asked how they could do nothing about the genocide going on around them. They responded that they did not know about the atrocities that were going on. They were unaware of the slaughter of people being perpetrated by their own government. They had been too busy singing in their churches, or being distracted by the other realities of life, to notice.

Fewer than 10% of the German population belonged to the Nazi Party. Ten million people were killed without anyone noticing, and without anyone standing up for those being killed. After the war, the Germans claimed they knew nothing of the concentration camps, or the killings.

The agenda of death has a way of convincing those around it that either it does not exist, or that it is necessary for the "good of the community."

It is easy for tyranny to gain control of a society when the people are either distracted, or unwilling to admit that the atrocities being committed exist. We even get to the point where we want to refuse to admit that our society could commit such atrocities, and to aid us in drowning out the truth, we decide to sing just a little louder.

In the end, a new and glorious future cannot be reached by way of murder. Our children are supposed to be a blessing, yet millions upon millions have been killed in the womb, and discarded as if their lives are unimportant, or an inconvenience. But, as with anything, the pushing of the envelope does not stop at abortion. It began with first trimester abortions. Full term abortion has now become a subject of debate, and it won't be long before we become like Rome during the empire's darkest days, and the killing of a child up to the age of two will be legal. Evil never contains itself, or is satisfied with a limited amount of innocent blood.

That is where we must come into the fight. Through Christ, it is our duty to resist evil, and to stand up for those that are unable to stand up for themselves. To stop the genocide, it will take revolution, an awakening of God's people, and active involvement in resolving the issue through activity, education, and prayer.

As a nation, we have traded morality, and called it a woman's reproductive right. The bodies of babies are piling up while we lose argument after argument in the court system. In some cases, we have determined that we have lost, that there is nothing we can do to stop the slaughter of innocent lives. We have accepted the will of *the well-funded* over our own convictions, and as we look to our future, the reality is, there are many lives that were supposed to be a part of that future that now never will.

We would have made great Nazis. Through our silence, or our loud singing in the face of genocide, we have put on the uniforms, turned our heads, and have allowed the lives of millions to be destroyed. Genocide is not just something that tyrannical systems did in history. It's right here, in our country.

People ask, "How could the German people know nothing of millions of innocent human beings being murdered? How could they claim they weren't involved? What causes people to deny their own history?"

History is repeating itself. Are we going to deny what happened? Or, are we going to realize that we are all responsible for what happens in our society? Should we blindly follow a system the kills our children, while justifying the slaughter as being a "right?" Or do we understand that God would never sanction such a thing, so it cannot be a right?

Abortion is death, and the death of the innocent in such a brutal manner is the height of evil. Darkness, however, never reveals itself as darkness, but as an angel of light, or in the case of abortion, as a woman's "reproductive right."

In the film, *The Usual Suspects* (1995), the character being played by Kevin Spacey made a very interesting, and accurate, observation. He said, "The greatest trick the devil ever pulled was convincing the world he didn't exist."

The second greatest trick Satan has ever pulled has been to convince an entire population that killing their own, innocent children, while the babies develop in the womb, is not evil.

12 – Revolution

To end abortion, it will take a Revolution of information, and activity.

You are the revolution.

BIBLIOGRAPHY

40 Days for Life. November 9, 2014.
 <http://40daysforlife.com/>.

"Abortion Methods." *Society for the Protection of Unborn Children*. November 13, 2014.
 <https://www.spuc.org.uk/education/abortion/meth ods>.

"Abortions in America." *Operation Rescue*. November 9, 2014. <http://www.operationrescue.org/about-abortion/abortions-in-america/>.

Aguilar, Merilida. "My testimony: You Stomping Ground, Bound4Life Salinas." *Bound4Life*. September 26, 2014. November 13, 2014.
 <http://bound4life.com/blog/2014/09/26/your-stomping-ground-bound4life-salinas/>.

Allahpundit. "Gosnell abortion-clinic worker: One of the babies 'sounded like a little alien.'" *Hot Air*. April 9, 2013. November 9, 2014.
 <http://hotair.com/archives/2013/04/09/gosnell-abortion-clinic-worker-one-of-the-babies-sounded-like-a-little-alien/>.

Andrew M. Allison, Mr. Richard Maxfield, K. Delynn Cook, and W. Cleon Skousen, *The Real Thomas Jefferson*; New York: National Center for Constitutional Studies (2009).

Articles of Confederation, March 1, 1781; *http://avalon.law.yale.edu/18th_century/artconf.asp*

Birth Choice: Real Answers, Real Help. November 9, 2014. <http://www.birthchoice.net/>.

Birth Choice: Temecula. November 9, 2014. < http://birthchoicetemecula.com/>.

"Body Parts on Shelves at Gruesome Abortion Mill." *CBS News.* January 20, 2011. November 12, 2014. <http://www.cbsnews.com/news/body-parts-on-shelves-at-gruesome-abortion-mill/>.

Chapman, Michael W. "NYC: More Black Babies Killed by Abortion Than Born." *CNSNews.* February 20, 2014. November 9, 2014. <http://www.cnsnews.com/news/article/michael-w-chapman/nyc-more-black-babies-killed-abortion-born>.

Collins, Phillip D. "Engineering Evolution: The Alchemy of Eugenics." *Hospice Patients Alliance.* January 10, 2005. November 9, 2014. <http://www.hospicepatients.org/alchemy-eugenics.html>.

Corona Life Services. November 9, 2014. < http://clspregnancy.com/>.

"Doctor Kermit Gosnell found guilty of murdering infants in late-term abortions." Fox News. January 12, 2015.
<http://www.foxnews.com/us/2013/05/13/jury-split-on-2-counts-in-trial-abortion-doctor-kermit-gosnell/>

EMC Front Line Pregnancy Centers. November 9, 2014. < http://www.emcfrontline.org/>.

Ertelt, Steven. "Expert Tells Congress Unborn Babies Can Feel Pain Starting at 8 Weeks." *LifeNews.* May 23, 2013. November 9, 2014.
<http://www.lifenews.com/2013/05/23/expert-tells-congress-unborn-babies-can-feel-pain-starting-at-8-weeks/>.

Ertelt, Steven. "Media Ignores Abortion Doc Who Killed Babies With His Bare Hands." *LifeNews.* May 16, 2013. November 15, 2014.
<http://www.lifenews.com/2013/05/16/media-ignores-abortion-doc-who-killed-babies-with-his-bare-hands/>.

"Exposing the Shameful Link Between Abortion, Racism, and Eugenics." *JHOP San Diego.* 2009. November 12, 2014.
<http://www.jhopgear.jhopsd.com/articles/morality-and-culture/164-exposing-the-shameful-link-between-abortion-racism-and-eugenics>.

Forsythe, Clark. "Pro-Lifers Must be Realistic About How, When Roe Abortion Case Can be Reversed." *LifeNews* September 16, 2009. November 9, 2014.
<http://www.lifenews.com/2009/09/16/nat-5475/>.

Green, Jewels. "Former abortion worker: my sleep was haunted by dismembered children." *LifeSite*. December 20, 2011. November 12, 2014. <https://www.lifesitenews.com/news/former-abortion-worker-my-sleep-was-haunted-by-tiny-limbless-phantom-babies>.

Green, Jewels. "Pro-Abortion Propaganda." *Live Action*. August 14, 2011. November 12, 2014. <http://liveaction.org/blog/pro-abortion-propaganda/>.

"Gruesome: Bodies of aborted children trafficked from Canada and incinerated for electricity at Oregon plant." *"Catholic Online."* April 24, 2014. November 12, 2014. <http://www.catholic.org/news/international/americas/story.php?id=55109>.

Hampson, Rick. "Gruesome testimony renews debate over abortion." *USA TODAY*. April 22, 2013. November 12, 2014. <http://www.usatoday.com/story/news/nation/2013/04/22/gosnell-abortion-trial/2100103/>.

Hayford, Jack, ed., "Kingdom Dynamics: Is Abortion Wrong?, Godliness and Moral Purity." *New Spirit-Filled Life Bible: Kingdom Equipping Through the Power of the Word – New King James Version.* Nashville: Thomas Nelson Publishers, 1982. 793. Print.

Healthwise Staff. "Manual and Vacuum Aspiration for Abortion." *WebMD*. August 31, 2012. November 12, 2014. <http://www.webmd.com/women/manual-and-vacuum-aspiration-for-abortion>.

Hinkle, Linda. "When Does an Unborn Baby Have a Heartbeat?" *LiveStrong*. August 16, 2013. November 9, 2014. <http://www.livestrong.com/article/242600-when-does-an-unborn-baby-have-a-heartbeat/>.

Hogan, Carol. "Forty-Four Years of Legalized Abortion in California." *California Catholic Conference*. June 2011. November 9, 2014. <http://www.cacatholic.org/index.php/issues2/rever ence-for-life/respect-life/91-forty-four-years-of-legalized-abortion-in-california>.

Jenkins, Colleen. "U.S. court strikes down North Carolina ultrasound abortion law." *Reuters/Yahoo News*. December 22, 2014. January 12, 2015. <http://news.yahoo.com/court-strikes-down-north-carolina-ultrasound-abortion-law-175812728.html>

"Justice for Trayvon. What About Justice for Tonya?" *Too Many Aborted*. January 12, 2015. <http://www.toomanyaborted.com/justice-4-tonya/>

Kengor, Paul and Clark Doerner, Patricia. "Reagan's Darkest Hour." *National Review Online*. January 22, 2008. November 9, 2014. <http://www.nationalreview.com/articles/223437/re agans-darkest-hour/paul-kengor>.

"Kermit Gosnell and his House of Horrors." *Too Many Aborted*. January 12, 2015. <http://www.toomanyaborted.com/gosnell/>

Klein, Aaron. "Sunstein: Fetuses 'use' women, abortion limits 'troublesome.'" *World Net Daily*. September 25, 2009. November 9, 2014. <http://www.wnd.com/2009/09/110934/>.

"Legal History of Abortion (1821-Present)". *Students for Life of America Law Students*. November 9, 2014. <http://law.studentsforlife.org/legalities-of-abortion/>.

Locke, John. *An Essay Concerning Human Understanding*. Glasgow: R. Griffin and Co., 1836. E-book.

"Margaret Sanger: Founder of Planned Parenthood – In Her Own Words". *Diane Dew dot com*. 2001. November 9, 2014. <http://www.dianedew.com/sanger.htm>.

Mr. Conservative. "Abortion Workers Recall Stitching Together Gruesome Body Parts Of Killed Babies." *MRConservative*. August 7, 2013. November 12, 2014. <http://mrconservative.com/2013/08/22522-abortion-workers-recall-stitching-together-gruesome-body-parts-of-killed-babies/>.

"Planned Parenthood". *Black Genocide dot org.* November 9, 2014. <http://blackgenocide.org/planned.html>.

"Planned Parenthood's Racism". *Life Research Institute.* June 1994. November 9, 2014. <http://www.ewtn.com/library/prolife/ppracism.txt>.

Pregnancy Information. *Baby2See.* November 9, 2014. <http://www.baby2see.com/index.html>.

"Ronald Reagan on Abortion." *On The Issues.* November 9, 2014. <http://www.ontheissues.org/celeb/Ronald_Reagan_Abortion.htm>.

Scheidler, Eric. "Accomplishment #1: Countless babies have been saved by pro-life witness on the street." *Life Site News.* February 4, 2013. November 9, 2014. <https://www.lifesitenews.com/blogs/accomplishment-1-countless-babies-have-been-saved-by-pro-life-witness-on-th>.

Sing a Little Louder. January 12, 2015. <http://singloudermovie.com/>

"Society for Humane Abortion. Records, 1962-1979 (inclusive), 1963-1975 (bulk): A Finding Aide." *Harvard University Library, Radcliffe College* August 1979. November 9, 2014. <http://oasis.lib.harvard.edu/oasis/deliver/~sch00916>.

Stanton Health Care. November 9, 2014. <http://www.stantonhealthcare.org/>.

Terzo, Sarah. "Aborted babies die with their arms around each other." *ClinicQuotes*. August 7, 2014. November 14, 2014. <http://clinicquotes.com/aborted-babies-die-with-their-arms-around-each-other/>.

Terzo, Sarah. "Abortion worker quits: can't keep looking at "baby's body parts." *ClinicQuotes*. August 5, 2014. November 14, 2014. <http://clinicquotes.com/abortion-worker-quits-cant-keep-looking-at-babys-body-parts

Terzo, Sarah. "Medical Student: Abortion is 'Invasive' and 'Gruesome.'" *ClinicQuotes*. September 21, 2012. November 14, 2014. <http://clinicquotes.com/medical-student-abortion-is-invasive-and-gruesome/>.

Terzo, Sarah. "Partial-birth abortion horror revisited: nurse tells grisly tale of the procedure." *Live Action News*. April 7, 2014. January 12, 2015. <http://liveactionnews.org/partial-birth-abortion-horror-revisited-nurse-tells-grisly-tale-of-the-procedure/>

Terzo, Sarah. "Pro-choice woman talks about her "brutal" abortion experience." *Live Action News*. July 4, 2014. January 12, 2015. <http://liveactionnews.org/pro-choice-woman-talks-about-her-brutal-abortion-experience/>

The Constitution of the United States, with Index, and The Declaration of Independence. Washington D.C.: National Center for Constitutional Studies, 2013. iii, v-vi. Print.

"The Immigration Act of 1924 (The Johnson-Reed Act)." *U.S. Department of State, Office of the Historian.* November 9, 2014. <https://history.state.gov/milestones/1921-1936/immigration-act>.

"The Negro Project." *Too Many Aborted.* November 9, 2014. <http://www.toomanyaborted.com/thenegroproject>.

"Timeline of abortion laws and events." *Chicago Tribune.* November 9, 2014. <http://www.chicagotribune.com/sns-abortion-timeline-story.html>.

"TX abortionist impales, twists heads off live babies." *Jill Stanek.* January 12, 2015. < http://www.jillstanek.com/2013/05/breaking-photos-tx-abortionist-impales-twists-heads-off-live-babies/>

Vespa, Matt. "Kermit Gosnell Trial: He Isn't the Only One Conducting Gruesome Abortions." *News.Mic.* April 28, 2013. November 12, 2014. <http://mic.com/articles/38413/kermit-gosnell-trial-he-isn-t-the-only-one-conducting-gruesome-abortions>.

Wetzstein, Cheryl. "Gruesome picture puts new pressure on China over one-child policy." Washington Times. July 9, 2012. November 14, 2014. <http://www.washingtontimes.com/news/2012/jul/9/gruesome-picture-puts-new-pressure-on-china-over-o/>.

ABOUT THE AUTHOR

Douglas V. Gibbs is a radio host on KCAA AM1050, and KMET AM1490. He blogs at www.politicalpistachio.com, and is the author of *25 Myths of the United States Constitution*, and *The Basic Constitution: An Examination of the Principles and Philosophies of the United States Constitution*. He is a public speaker on a variety of topics, all of them discussed through the lens of the United States Constitution. Doug is an instructor, hosting Constitution Classes in Temecula, and Corona, California, as well as for *Constitution Education Seminars*. Nationally, Douglas V. Gibbs is known as an authority regarding the original intent of the United States Constitution, and he has discussed his views regarding the Constitution on television outlets, including Fox News, One America News, Al Jazeera America, MSNBC, NBC, CBS, ABC, ARD German Television, and various other smaller outlets. He has also been interviewed on the radio for National Public Radio, and various stations around the country. Doug is a free lance newspaper columnist for The Central Idaho Post. His articles have appeared on websites like, but not limited to, The Free Republic, Drudge

Report, Canada Free Press, Conservative Crusader, Conservative Action Alerts, Conservative Network News, Christian Response Alerts, Flash Point 2016, Before It's News, Insight on Freedom, Omega Dispatch, and The Examiner. He has been featured on the American Family Association's OneNewsNow news portal a number of times. Doug is a member of the California Republican Assembly, "Unite Inland Empire" patriot group coalition, the "American Authors Association", the "Committee of Concerned Journalists" and "The Military Writers Society of America." He received the Golden Anchor Award for his patriotic commentary in 2008, was a candidate for his local Murrieta City Council in 2010, and was awarded a California State Senate Certificate of Recognition in 2014. Doug is a family man, married thirty years to his high school sweetheart. He is the father of two and has six grandchildren. Doug is a proud United States Navy veteran.

Douglas V. Gibbs may be contacted for comment, if you would like to become a sponsor on his radio programs or for his events, if you would like to hire Doug to be a speaker at an event, or if you would like him to conduct a seminar or Constitution class, at *douglasvgibbs@reagan.com*.

Made in the USA
Middletown, DE
08 September 2019